# CIRCULAR

## TO SUPERINTENDENTS OF CANAL REPAIRS.

CANAL DEPARTMENT,
*Albany, March*, 1854.

*To the Superintendents of Canal Repairs on the New-York State Canals.*

It has been usual hitherto to issue circular letters from this department explanatory of your duties, in order that you may thereby, to a certain extent at least, be informed of what will be expected of you by this department. In preparing the following instructions I have to a great extent adopted those of my predecessors, varying them where it appeared necessary to conform to changes in the laws and duties of your office.

Section 1, chapter 57, of the Laws of 1851 expressly provides that "Superintendents appointed by the canal board on the several canals of this state shall give their *personal* and *constant* attention to the duties of their office."

It is not competent for you, therefore, to perform your duties by proxy, or to be engaged in any other business that requires your personal attention. It is an office that requires vigilance and activity. The interests committed to your care are great, and a little negligence on your part may be the cause of great damage. You will do great injustice, therefore, to the state, and yourself also, if you assume to enter upon the duties without a firm determination to give the state your prompt, energetic and undivided attention to the duties of your office.

It is made your duty as such superintendent, under the direction of the canal commissioners, and particularly of the commissioner who has charge of the line of the canal on which you are employed, to keep in good repair the canal and the public works committed to your charge; and you are, under the advice and direction of the commissioner, to make all necessary contracts in the manner hereinafter stated for that purpose, and faithfully to expend all such moneys as shall be placed in your hands by the canal commissioners and the auditor. Sections 99, 100, 101, 102 and 103, on page 236, vol. 1 of the first edition of the Revised Statutes, contain an enumeration of some of the most important of your duties, and I therefore copy them at large.

"§ 99. Each superintendent of repairs, and every collector of tolls, before he shall enter on his official duties, shall execute and file in the office of the auditor a bond for the faithful execution of his trust, in such penalty and form as the canal board shall direct, and with such sureties as the auditor shall approve.

"§ 100. It shall be the duty of each superintendent, under the direction of the canal commissioners, to keep in repair such sections of the canals and works connected therewith, as shall be committed to his charge ; to make all necessary contracts for that purpose, and faithfully to expend all such moneys as shall be placed in his hands by the canal commissioners or the commissioners of the canal fund.

"§ 101. Each superintendent shall be under the direction of the canal commissioners, and especially of the acting commissioner having charge of the line of the canal on which such superintendent is employed.

"§ 102. Each superintendent shall, as often as once in sixty days, render his account to the auditor, who shall audit the same ; and if any superintendent shall omit to render his account, or his account as rendered be not satisfactory, the auditor shall notify the canal board and the commissioners of the canal fund thereof, and no further advances of money shall be made to such superintendent, but he shall be immediately removed from office.

"§ 103. Before any superintendent's account for expenditures shall be presented to the auditor, the canal commissioner having charge of that part of the canal on which such superintendent is employed shall certify, on such account, that he has examined the same ; that the several disbursements, specified therein, were made under his direction on the canal, or for repairs necessary to be made thereon ; and that he believes such disbursements to be proper and reasonable, and to have been made as charged."

You are under the necessity, from time to time, of purchasing materials and employing hands for the repair of the canal ; and as it is and always has been the policy of the state to pay as soon as the materials are furnished or the service rendered, provision has been made to place money at the disposal of the superintendent for this purpose. The 7th and 8th sections of "An act in relation to the canals," passed May 16, 1837, provide as follows:

"§ 7. Before any advance of money shall be made to a superintendent of canal repairs, by the auditor, he shall make out a detailed statement, in such form as the auditor shall prescribe, of the several anticipated objects of expenditure on the line of canal under his charge.

"§ 8. If the said estimate shall be filed in the office of the auditor, with the certificate thereon of the canal commissioner, stating that in his opinion the whole amount, or if less than the whole amount, what portion of the said estimate should be advanced, the auditor may make advances on the same, in such sums and as often as he may deem necessary ; provided such advances shall not exceed the amount certified by the commissioner."

This money is to be advanced to you on satisfactory evidence that it is required for the repair of the public works. And in order that the auditor may have a reasonable foundation for an opinion that the advance asked for by the superintendent is "required in the execution of his duties," it is necessary that you should, previous to asking for such advance, carefully examine every part of your line of the canal, and make out a full and detailed statement of all the repairs required to be made, and the sums which, in your judgment, it will be necessary to expend upon them for the ensuing sixty days. In this estimate the location and character of the work, on which the expenditure is to be made, should be given with such minuteness and precision as to enable the commissioner to trace every dollar of the public money to some portion of the public work.

1. If a bridge is to be repaired or rebuilt, the estimate should give the expense of removing the old and preparing for the new foundation, the quantity and cost of the stone and lime, the expense of the mason work, the quantity and cost of the timber, the planks, the board, the iron work, &c. If an aqueduct, a culvert, a lock, or any other structure, requires to be repaired or rebuilt, its location should be given, and a minute estimate made of the kind, quantity and cost of the different materials necessary to be used. If there are materials on hand suitable for the contemplated work, the quantity and the amount paid for the materials on hand should be stated, and deducted from the estimated cost of the structure.

2. The same particulars should be given in relation to each repair which has been commenced and remains unfinished.

3. The tools, implements and apparatus to be purchased, and their probable cost.

4. The sum necessary to pay lock-tenders, according to the contracts with them for their wages, expense of lamps, &c.

5. The sum necessary to be paid during the 60 days to each contractor on your line.

6. If the tow-path is to be raised, or any work is to be performed which is not contracted for, the location and character of the work should be given, with a detailed estimate of the expense of doing it.

The estimated expenditure upon each bridge, culvert, &c., should be shown separately, and the total sum required for the sixty days should be given in a general footing.

By chapter 16 of the Laws passed at the present session of the Legislature, the canal commissioners are authorized and required to adopt immediate measures to bottom out the narrow and crooked portions of the Erie, Oswego, and Cayuga and Seneca canals, so as to admit the passage of boats of the enlarged size at the earliest possible period, drawing three and one-half feet of water. The estimate for all work you are directed by the commissioner in charge to do under this law, you will show separately in your detailed estimate. The regulations prescribed for the estimate under the act of 1847 is as follows:

"That every superintendent of repairs on the canal, in order to obtain an advance of moneys to be expended on the canal, shall make out a detailed statement of the several objects of expenditure for the next sixty days, so far as he can anticipate the same, stating whether for building bridges, repairing aqueducts, graveling the tow-path, the pay of lock-tenders, teams and laborers, the purchase of materials, tools and the like, and may add to the estimate a separate sum for contingencies, and shall deliver two copies of the said estimate to the canal commissioner. On one of the said copies the commissioner shall certify what amount in his opinion ought to be advanced, which estimate and certificate shall be filed in the canal department, on receiving the balance; the other copy of the estimate shall be retained by the commissioner, to be used on the settlement of the accounts of the superintendent at the end of sixty days."

You are required to open an account as superintendent, and separate and distinct from your individual concerns, with some bank, in which the advances made to you by the auditor of the canal department are to be deposited.

You will be furnished by the bank where you keep your account with a check and bank book, the latter of which you are required to have written up at least once a month. The check book you will of course confine to your account as superintendent; and by entering in it, upon the blank margin opposite to the check, the sums advanced to you from time to time, you will be able at any moment to tell the amount you have in bank.

The payments which you are to make upon your line of canal may be classed under five general heads, viz:

1st. Payments to lock-tenders, which are in each case for a price certain for a month, or for two months, and the total amount of which for those periods can almost always be known with precision.

2d. Payments to regular and permanent hands under foremen who keep check rolls, and the amount necessary to pay whom for a month can, by information from the foreman a few days before the close of each month, be told with almost as much accuracy as that of the lock-tenders.

3d. Payment for materials for repairs, including payments on contract.

4th. Payments for tools, &c., being mostly merchants' and smiths' bills.

5th. Miscellaneous payments.

By a compliance with the requirements of this circular, you will always have it in your power to have to your credit, in the bank where you shall keep your account, funds sufficient for the necessary expenditures on your line of canal. And while provision is thus made for your public expenses, which will prevent the necessity of your ever having recourse to your individual credit to meet them, you will consider the funds so placed at your disposal as sacred to the uses of the canal, and that they are to be drawn from the bank no faster and in no larger sums than the necessity of payments absolutely requires. Thus, in relation to the payments of the 1st and 2d class, it is not conceived to be necessary that the moneys to make them monthly, which is as often as they will be made, need be drawn by you from the bank until near the expiration of the month in which the service shall be performed.

Payments of the 3d class and their amount cannot be anticipated with equal precision, but they can sufficiently so to render it unnecessary that you should have any considerable sum in your hands at once to meet them.

Payments of the 4th class are generally delayed by the superintendent until the close of the sixty days. Those with whom you deal to any extent, and with whom you have a running account, if they are certain of receiving their pay at the end of sixty days, would willingly delay presenting their bills until that time. Thus payments of this class will not, generally speaking, have to be made until the close of the two months.

For payments of the 5th class, as they cannot be foreseen, and for such of those under the other heads as are of the same character, you will of course have to be provided with funds in your hands to the necessary amount.

The canal moneys being on interest in the deposit banks, it is expected that a superintendent will not make his drafts any oftener, nor in larger amounts, than a just regard to the public wants shall render necessary.

It is supposed, as a general rule, that not more than one-fourth part of a certified advance will be wanted by a superintendent before the middle of the first month, one-fourth part at the close of the month, one-fourth part by the middle of the second month, and the residue at the close of that month. By this manner of drawing for the advance, a superintendent never need be subjected to any delay in making his payments, if his estimate be duly filed in this department, as his deposit bank will always be willing to take his drafts on the auditor.

The proportions of the advance, and the periods when to be drawn for, may be varied by circumstances; and should it be necessary to draw for a much larger proportion of the advance, at any one time, than as above specified, *a letter containing the reasons therefor* should be written in time to be received here previous to the presentation of the draft for payment.

By a resolution of the canal board, no superintendent of repairs is allowed to keep his official account at a bank which shall advance to him moneys beyond the amount for which the bank shall have advice from the auditor that the superintendent's drafts on the auditor will be paid.

The bank account of a superintendent, in his official capacity, being considered by the canal board, as it is in fact, a public account, the bank will be required by the auditor to render to him from time to time a copy of it, as the banks in which collectors make their deposits are required to do by law. The form of keeping the account is prescribed by the auditor. It will be required to show, on the one side, the amount and date of each draft drawn by the superintendent on the auditor; and on the other, the date of the payment of each check, its No., its date, and the name of the person in whose favor it is drawn.

To enable superintendents to comply with all the requirements of this circular, the canal board have authorized the commissioner to allow you such an amount for clerk hire as in his opinion shall be necessary.

This will enable you to keep the necessary accounts, and to make the prescribed estimates, reports and contracts, and the necessary copies thereof.

By keeping a separate account with every contract, with every lock-tender, and with every separate job of work, such as a bridge, a lock, a culvert, an aqueduct, in which each structure shall be charged with the quantity and cost of the stone, lime, timber, &c.; excavation, embankment, mason work, carpenter work, iron, &c., &c., and also by keeping the check book or cash account, the bank book, &c., as required in the preceding part of this circular, you will be enabled at any time during the second month, by a careful examination of all these accounts and of all the work which is going on under your supervision, to form an accurate estimate of the sum required to close up your accounts at the end of the sixty days. This examination should be made several days before the close of the second month, and in time, if it becomes necessary, to write to and get an answer from the auditor, previous to the close of the two months.

If you ascertain that you have money enough to pay all claims against you as the agent of the state, up to the time at which you are required to render your accounts, it will not be necessary for you to pursue the course hereinafter prescribed; but if on examination you find that the money to pay off the claims at the end of the sixty days will fall short, you should satisfy the commissioner of the situation of your accounts and money, and obtain from him the usual certificate for a further advance, to enable you to close up your accounts. When you ask this certificate of the commissioner, you should exhibit to him your bank account, and your expenditures, and such estimate as will enable the commissioner to judge of the necessity of the advance.

You are not to pay out the public money without taking a receipt, dated at the time of payment; you are not, under any pretence whatever, to take a receipt without paying the money to the full amount of the receipt taken. You are not in any case to give notes or due-bills to any person who has furnished materials or rendered service to the state.

A mode of transacting business, which will only be practiced by those who wish to speculate on the public money, instead of paying it to those who have earned it, must eventually result either in a fraud upon the treasury or upon the individual who signs the receipt. To prevent either of these results, each superintendent is required to make oath that the money has actually been paid for every receipt which he asks to have credited to his account.

In the Laws of 1851, chapter 57, section 2, it is enacted that "No superintendent, appointed as aforesaid, shall under any pretence whatever take a receipt for labor done, services performed or materials furnished for the canals, when the money shall not be actually paid."

And in the 1st section of chapter 310 of the Laws of 1842, it is expressly required that "proof in some apt form shall be furnished on oath that it [the voucher] was so filled up at the time it was taken, and that the money, mentioned therein to have been paid, was in fact paid in cash or by draft on some specified bank."

Every voucher taken by a disbursing officer should contain a brief and true history of the transaction between the agent of the state and the individual who signs the voucher; if it is for labor, the account should give the number of days and the date of commencing and ending; the price per day or month; and if the voucher covers the services of any person who does not sign the receipt, the account should give such explanation as to show that the person signing the receipt had a legal right to receive and receipt for the money. For instance, if a man is employed with his son, who is a minor, or with an apprentice, the fact should be stated, and the sum for the pay of the minor or apprentice carried out in a separate line, with the price per day or month. But in all other cases the money should be paid to and receipted by the person who does the labor; and in no case should one man be allowed to hire hands to labor for the state, and receive the pay for such labor. All laborers should be employed by the superintendent, and the money paid to the person thus employed, or to his written order, and not to any other person.

If a disbursing officer adheres strictly to the rule of embodying in each receipt the simple truth in relation to the transaction between the state and the person signing it, he cannot be embarrassed in the settlement of his accounts. Justifiable deviations from prescribed forms may be explained or excused; but deviations from fact in a voucher destroys its validity, and an explanation, by disclosing the real facts of the case, instead of excusing the officer, tends to cast suspicion either upon his integrity or his capacity. The practice of allowing a person hired by the month to receipt for a team driven by him, but which belongs to another person, is wrong, although the interests of the state may not be affected, for the simple reason that the voucher does not give a true relation of the transaction. Such a voucher, however, may be rendered valid by a writing from the owner of the team, authorizing the driver to receipt for the use of it.

To every voucher of merchants, mechanics, and miscellaneous accounts, in which are included articles purchased or services rendered, not paid for on delivery of articles or at time of rendition of service (and which is intended especially to include running accounts of every description), all accounts for labor not included in check rolls, all bills left unpaid by your predecessor, which you may be authorized or directed to pay, must be verified, before payment, before yourself or some officer authorized to administer oaths, which affidavit must be attached to the voucher and returned therewith to this department. The following form of affidavit has been prepared for such purpose. As it is desirable that at the expiration of each sixty days the department should be furnished with the full amount of expenditures during such period, there will be required in cases of all vouchers, including any item or charge accruing at a date anterior to the last abstract of expenditure, to be added to the affidavit a statement or explanation of the reasons why the same was not personally presented or paid:

State of New-York, } ss.<br>
*County of* ,

A. B. (or if a firm, say A. B., one of the firm of C. D. & Co., named in the annexed account), of , in the county of being duly sworn, saith that all the items in the annexed account are correct, and accrued at the dates respectively as stated therein; that no part of the same, or any item therein, is charged at more than its fair value; that it is a just claim against the State of New-York to the amount of dollars and cents, specified therein; that no part thereof hath been included in any former bill rendered against the state; that there are no legal or equitable offsets against the same; that the same, or any part thereof, hath not been paid to this deponent or any other person, by or in behalf of said state, to the knowledge, information or belief of this deponent; that this deponent is (or if a firm, say that the said firm are) the lawful owner of such account and entitled to the payment thereof. And further, that all the labor charged therein has been applied upon the works and to the benefit of the state; and that all the property charged therein has been delivered to the duly authorized agents of the state at and, according to the best of the knowledge, information and belief of this deponent, used for the benefit of the state by or under the direction of one of the authorized agents thereof.

### *Foremen and Rolls.*

Industrious and faithful men ought to be employed as foremen, on whose fidelity reliance can be placed to keep the roll with such accuracy as to do justice to the individual as well as to the state. The roll should be made up at the end of every month, and the number of days for which each person has labored should be carried out opposite his name, with the price per day or month, and the total sum due him; and the roll, thus made out, should be read in the hearing of each laborer, or at least the foreman should state to each laborer the number of days, the price, and the total sum entered on the roll opposite his name. When the roll is thus made out, and the sums footed up, the truth of it is to be verified by the oath of the foreman, in the following form:

STATE OF NEW-YORK, } *ss.*
*County of* , }

of , a foreman under , superintendent, being duly sworn, saith that the foregoing check roll, the total number of days' labor entered on which is , was kept by him as forman of the laborers and teams entered thereon; and that he has himself (and has good reason to believe that the several other persons and the teams entered upon the said roll have) performed the labor in the service of the state for the whole number of days and parts of days stated in said roll, and at the prices entered opposite each name and team respectively; and that the description of each work, and the number of days on each work, as entered on said check roll, is in all respects just and true, according to the best of his knowledge and belief.

A. B., *Foreman.*

Subscribed and sworn to, this }
day of , 185 , before me, }

C. D., *Superintendent of Canal Repairs.*

If the labor has not in all cases been performed under the inspection of the foreman, so as to enable him to swear positively that it has been done, he can make such exceptions as the case requires.

It is desirable that the oath be administered in all cases by the superintendent. If the superintendent is not present, the roll may be sworn to before any judge, justice or commissioner.

The roll being thus verified, you should yourself pay to each individual the sum due him according to the roll, and take his receipt therefor, which should be dated on the day of the transaction.

The receipts should be numbered, commencing with the first name on the roll for No. 1, and numbering them in the order in which the names stand on the roll. The receipts, when executed, should be filed on the outside, with the number, the name of the person giving the receipt, and the amount in each case. These receipts, without being folded, should be arranged according to their numbers, and carefully folded in the check roll, which should be filed on the outside of the roll, with the name of the foreman, the month embraced in the roll and the total amount paid on it.

This roll, covering the receipts of all the laborers under one foreman for a month, will occupy only one line, or the space of a single voucher, on the abstract of the superintendent, and will be numbered on the outside, with reference to the other vouchers entered upon the general abstract. The entries upon the check roll should be confined exclusively to the labor of the hands employed by the state, and the service of teams where they are furnished. The foreman and hands employed by the month are not allowed to furnish materials, and therefore the roll will be confined to their labor; and if the same individual who is temporarily employed with his team, has also an account for materials furnished, the receipt for the materials should be entered separately on the abstract of the superintendent.

Your accounts being prepared as before directed, and having made yourself sure that you have made all the payments and procured all the vouchers for the two months, you are to enter at the bottom of the abstract the one-sixth part of your salary, which you are to retain at the closing of each account. In this shape you are to lay the accounts before the canal commissioner upon your line, and his signature to the certificate, required from him, must be obtained before the accounts can be allowed, or even examined at this office. This should be done as soon after the close of each two months as is possible; and that you may be prepared to lay the accounts before the commissioner, without delay to him, you should have the vouchers taken and in order, and the abstract completed immediately after the expiration of the last month.

When all the vouchers and the amount of your salary for two months have been entered upon the abstract, and the general statement of your account is made, according to the form on the abstract annexed, the whole is to be verified by your oath, in the following form:

STATE OF NEW-YORK, } ss.
*County of* ,

, superintendent of canal repairs, having charge of the line of canal specified in the above abstract, doth solemnly swear that the foregoing is a true abstract of all the vouchers taken by him as such superintendent for the days ending on the day of , 185 ; and doth further swear that the money specified in the several receipts, of which the above is an abstract (except vouchers marked A paid by agent), has been actually paid, as specified in said receipts, in cash or by check on the bank; and further, that all the receipts, not specifically excepted, were each and every of them filled up as they now appear, before they were signed; and he doth further swear that, according to the best of his knowledge and belief, all the labor has been performed, services rendered and materials furnished for the benefit of the state, and the state alone, and at as fair and reasonable prices as the same could be procured; and further swears, that all fines, penalties, and forfeitures collected, and the sales of public property made, during the period aforesaid, on the line of canal under his charge, are, according to the best of his knowledge and belief, correctly entered on the said abstract.

Subscribed and sworn to before me, }
this day of 185 .

, *Commissioner.*

(In the absence of the commissioner, the oath may be taken before any judge, justice or commissioner.)

If from sickness, or any other cause, you are unable to go through your line and make the payments yourself, as you ought to do when you are able, you must then make such exceptions in the oath as the case requires, making a note on the back of each receipt, stating by whom the money was paid, and furnish an affidavit, to supply the deficiency, from the agent whom you shall have employed to go through the line for you and make the payments. Those who keep the rolls should not be furnished with money to pay the hands on their rolls. There have been abuses under this practice, which make it necessary to discontinue it, except in special cases; and then an explanation of the circumstances should be given to justify a deviation from the rule.

### *Report at the end of Sixty Days.*

At the close of the sixty days, in addition to the rolls of your foreman, and the receipts and abstract, you should prepare a full report, in the same order in which the estimate was made, showing the expenditure upon each structure, repair or job, and the separate cost of the labor and the different kinds of materials used, and the cost of all the materials furnished and work done on the line for the sixty days. If the cost of any culvert, bridge or other expenditure differs materially from the original estimate, the cause of such difference should be explained. Such report of expenditure should include all your expenditures during such sixty days; and no bills or accounts should be left unpaid to be included in any subsequent report.

All expenditures made by you under chapter 16 of the Laws of 1854, providing for the bottoming out of the narrow and crooked portions of the Erie, Oswego and Cayuga and Seneca canals, should be kept distinct, and shown separately in your detailed report and abstract. The report should be signed by you officially, be presented to the commissioner on the settlement of the account, and forwarded with the vouchers to this department.

*Purchases, by whom made.*

There has been a practice tolerated by some of the superintendents of allowing foremen, lock-tenders and others to make purchases on the credit of the state. All purchases should be made by the superintendent personally, or on his *written order*, and not otherwise. The superintendent is furnished with money to pay for everything which is required for the repair of the canals, and as soon as any work for the state is done, it should be promptly paid for; and at all events, the persons employed by the superintendent should not in any case be allowed to purchase articles for the canal on the credit of the state.

*Appointments of Subordinates.*

Chapter 57 of the Laws of 1851, section 3, confers upon you the power to appoint subordinates, and I therefore insert herein such section at large.

"Each superintendent so appointed shall have power to appoint his own foreman, lock-tenders and other subordinate persons necessary to enable him to discharge his official duties, and the compensation to each shall not exceed the rate of compensation established by the board of canal commissioners; but the canal commissioner in charge of any section of the canal in which any foreman, lock-tender or other subordinate person may be employed, or the board of canal commissioners, shall have absolute power to remove any foreman, lock-tender or other subordinate for misconduct, incompetency or neglect of duty, provided such canal commissioner or the board of canal commissioners making such removal shall specify the cause of such removal in writing, and file the same in the office of the auditor of the canal department within ten days from the date of such removal. In case of the removal of any such foreman, lock-tender or other subordinate, it shall be the duty of the commissioner or the board of canal commissioners making such removal immediately to notify the superintendent in charge of the section of the canal where such removal shall be made of the fact of such removal; and in case the superintendent shall neglect or refuse for three days to fill the vacancy thus created, and to notify the commissioner or board of canal commissioners thereof, it shall be the duty of the canal commissioner or the board of canal commissioners making such removal to fill such vacancy."

### *Lock Tenders.*

In the employment of lock-tenders, you should employ such men only as will give their personal attention to the business, and under no pretence should a contract for tending locks be made with a person who intends to sub-let or farm it out; and if any person, after his appointment as a lock-tender, does not give it his personal attention, or sub-lets or farms it out in any manner, you are required forthwith to remove him, and appoint another who will properly attend to his duties.

The lock-tender has the power of determining as to the preference between boats in passing a lock; and he ought not only to be in attendance himself, but he should be a sober, honest and discreet man, who can be relied upon to decide these questions promply and impartially.

Lock-tenders are prohibited, by a resolution of the canal board, from being concerned in any grocery on or near the canal. You are particularly required to see that this resolution is strictly complied with.

It is alleged that some of the lock-tenders on the canal have been in the practice of receiving presents of wood, &c., from boatmen; and it is inferred that those who receive such favors, repay them by giving to such persons an undue preference at the lock. The lock-tender should in no case place himself in a position which will expose him to the suspicion, on the part of a boatman against whom he may decide, that his decision is influenced by any benefits conferred by the person in whose favor he may decide. The practice alluded to is as objectionable as it would be for a magistrate on the trial of a suit between two neighbors to receive a present from either of the parties; a right decision, under such circumstances, would not protect the magistrate from the suspicion that his mind was biased by the favor conferred; at least this would be the opinion of the defeated party, under a feeling that his cause was a just one.

Every suit commenced by a lock-tender should be immediately reported to the superintendent; and all fines collected should be accounted for at the close of each month, and the particulars of each case should be entered in the books of the superintendent, and the moneys received should be accounted for in his first settlement after the transaction.

If any suit is to be carried to a higher court, the particulars of the case should be reported to the auditor in the same manner as is required in relation to suits commenced by the superintendent himself.

As soon as the lock-tenders are appointed on your line, you are requested to send a list of their names to the auditor, the number of the lock or locks in charge of each, the pay per month or the amount of the contract with each person. This will enable the auditor to estimate how much you require per month for lock-tending, and when you require it, as payment can only be necessary monthly.

### *Contracts.*

All contracts for materials or jobs made by you should be in writing, and duly executed by the parties, and an account opened in each case on the books of the superintendent; no contract should be made or important improvement undertaken by you without the express approval and ratification of the commissioner, and such approval or ratification of a contract should be signified by a certificate or endorsement on the contract. As soon as the contract is executed, notice should be given to the auditor, stating the substance of the contract, the name of the contractor, and such particulars as will enable the auditor to form an estimate of the amount of money required to complete the payments on the contract ; and the contract itself should be sent to the auditor, with the voucher for the first payment under it. If other payments are to be made on the same contract, the superintendent can retain a copy of it for his use. The return alluded to will aid the auditor in determining, when an advance is asked for, whether it is required to meet engagements made on behalf of the state.

You are prohibited by a resolution of the canal board from participating in any contract on the canals. This prohibition extends to all materials, tools or implements for the use of the canals, or any transaction by which you shall directly or indirectly be benefited by any of the money disbursed by you as superintendent. You cannot properly allow any contractor to take timber or materials from your land and receive a compensation therefor; and you should not do indirectly, through any relatives or friends, what you are not allowed to do directly by the law, the regulations and your instructions.

So far as you have it in your power, you should extend the same prohibition to your foremen, lock-tenders and all other persons employed by you on the state work. You should make no contracts with those who are employed in the service of the state, by the month or any fixed period, for the supply of materials in repairing the canal. Any bargain of this kind, on the part of a lock-tender or a foreman, is entirely inconsistent with his previous contract, to give the state his whole service as such foreman, lock-tender or laborer.

The fact has been disclosed, on the trial of one superintendent, that persons who were paid almost constantly for serving the state, were at the same time used as the instruments in buying off bidders for a contract, and getting possession of a job under a higher bid; thus depredating upon the state instead of serving it faithfully, as they were bound to do while they were retained from month to month, if not from year to year, in its service.

All contracts for repairs or improvements, directed by the Legislature or the canal board, must be made in writing, and public notice must be given that sealed proposals will be received for entering into such contracts. The ordinary repairs of the canal may be made without a special contract. But in all cases where the execution of a job, not directed by the Legislature or the canal board, can as conveniently be done by contract as those improvements which are thus directed, the state should have the benefit of the competition provided for in the law.

It is considered that all work which is susceptible of measurement should be done by written contracts, at specified prices. Sufficient public notice should be given for sealed proposals for all contracts, and in such manner as the commissioner may from time to time direct.

The canal commissioners, by section 1 of chapter 363 of the Laws of 1849, are authorized to direct you to purchase materials and tools for the ordinary repairs of the canals without advertising for the same, whenever, in their opinion, the interests of the state will be promoted thereby. But unless you have such express authority and direction from the commissioner, you are bound to procure the same under a contract, entered into in pursuance of the provisions of chapter 278 of the Laws of 1847.

The canal board, under the provisions of the law of 1847, have prescribed regulations relative thereto; but since the adoption of such regulations it has been provided, by section 1, chapter 363 of the Laws of 1849, that canal commissioners shall not be bound to accept proposals unless they deem it for the interests of the state; and you are, therefore, in no case to enter into the contract without first submitting it to the commissioner for his approval.

The following are the regulations adopted by the canal board on the 9th day of June, 1847, under the law of that year, also referred to:

"It shall be the duty of the superintendents of repairs, at least once in every six months, to make an estimate and statement in detail of the number and value of the boats, wheel-barrows, tools and other implements of every description, the quantity of the several kinds of timber, plank and boards, the number of pounds of iron, the kind and number of cubic yards of stone, and the quantity of all other materials which in their opinion will be required for the ordinary repairs of their respective sections during the six months for which the estimate is intended to provide, specifying the purposes, the number and location of the several structures, and the quantity required for each, and present the same to the commissioner in special charge of the division of the canals embracing said sections respectively; and on obtaining from the commissioner his certificate that the quantity and kind of materials, tools and other implements embraced in the statement so presented, or, after the same may have been modified by him, will in his opinion be necessary for the repairs of such section of the canal during the time specified in said estimate, the superintendent shall immediately give public notice of the kind, quantity and description of the materials, tools and other implements required, the place or places at which they are to be delivered, by publishing the same two successive weeks in two papers designated to publish the laws in each county through which the canal or section of the canal passes, specifying in said public notice the time and place, which shall be as nearly central on the section as may be, at which sealed proposals will be received for procuring and delivering said materials, tools and other implements.

"The notice will be in the following form:

"Proposals will be received by the undersigned, superintendent of canal repairs on the section of the canal, until Thursday, the day of next, at ten o'clock in the forenoon of that day, at the house of , in the town of , for procuring and delivering the following materials and tools, at the time and place below specified, viz:

MATERIALS.

| Quantity. | Kinds of material. | Quality of material. | Dimensions. | | | Place of delivery. | Time of delivery. |
|---|---|---|---|---|---|---|---|
| | | | Length in feet. | Breadth in inches. | Depth in inches. | | |
| | | | | | | | |

TOOLS, &c.

| Quantity. | Name of article. | Quality and description. | Place of delivery. | Time of delivery. |
|---|---|---|---|---|
| | | | | |

"Each proposition is to be sealed up, and to have endorsed on it 'Proposals for the supply of materials for repairs on the section of the Erie canal' [or for 'materials and tools,' or for boat, &c., according to the facts], and when thus sealed and endorsed, the proposition is to be put in an envelope, which is to be directed on the outside to the undersigned as canal superintendent in the town of The proposals will be opened in public, at the house of , in the town of , at the hour above stated.

"And then add as follows:

"Each offer must be accompanied by a written guarantee, signed by one or more responsible persons, and certified to be good by the supervisor of the town in which the bidder resides, to the effect that he or they undertake that the bidders will, if his or their bid be accepted, enter into an obligation, within ten days after the bidder or bidders shall have been notified personally or through the post-office of the acceptance of his or their bids, with good and sufficient sureties, to furnish the supplies proposed for.

"All propositions must be for a sum certain as to the price to be paid or received; and no proposition which is not thus definite and certain, or which contains any alternative condition or limitation as to price, can be received or acted on.

"No more than one proposition can be received from any one person for the same contract or object. Specifications and bills, also forms of bids and guarantees, will be furnished on application to the superintendent.

"Dated at , this day of , 185

"A. B., *Superintendent of Repairs.*

"The seals of the propositions should not be broken by the superintendent until the hour fixed in the advertisement for opening them ; and when the hour arrives, the bids should be opened publicly, and the seals should be broken in the presence of the bidders, if they desire to attend, and each person making a proposition should be permitted to examine the bid of any other person proposing for the same object or article. The superintendent should notify the acting commissioner in time to enable him to be present at the opening of the propositions; and if he cannot attend, notice should be given to the chief or resident engineer to be present.

"The original propositions and the certificate of the supervisor, with the guarantees in each case, shall be filed and preserved in the office of the superintendent.

"If bidders, to whom a contract is awarded, refuse to enter into it, and the superintendent has reason to suspect that the withdrawal is in consequence of a combination to get the contract on some of the bids less favorable to the interests of the state, he will at once give a second notice for propositions, as before. He may, however, enter into a contract with the bidder next most favorable to the interests of the state to those surrendered, provided he is furnished with the written permission of the commissioner in charge, and affidavits from all the contracting parties that no combination had been formed between themselves and the bidders who refused to contract, and that no compensation had been made or promised to them directly or indirectly by any of the contracting parties to induce them to withdraw, and that none of those who had withdrawn had or were to have any interest in the contract to be made, directly or indirectly; and all the papers required by this regulation should be carefully preserved in the office of the superintendent.

"As soon as the superintendent can decide who is entitled to the contracts, he should, if it meets with the approval of the commissioner, write on the propositions most favorable to the interests of the state, 'Accepted,' giving the date of the 'acceptance,' and sign the same as superintendent. This being done, written notice should be given to the person or persons making the proposition, to be signed by the superintendent and served personally by some person who will make affidavit of the service, or who will deposit the notice in the post-office, directed to the bidder, and make affidavit that he has done so.

"The following forms of propositions, and of the guarantee to accompany each, are to be used by the superintendents; and the blanks in the columns under the head of quantity, kind of material, quality, &c., and time and place of delivery, shall be filled by him, and given out on application to such person or persons as wish to make bids.

"PROPOSITION for procuring and delivering lumber and stone for the canal, all of which are to be of the quality and dimensions hereinafter stated, and in accordance with the bills and specifications this day exhibited:

| Quantity. | Kind of material. | Quality of materials. | Dimensions. | | | Price. | Amount. | Place to be delivered. | Time to be delivered. |
|---|---|---|---|---|---|---|---|---|---|
| | | | Length in feet | Breadth in inches. | Depth in inches. | | | | |
| Ft. B. M. | W. oak timber, | | | | | | | | |
| | " " plank, | | | | | | | | |
| | " pine timber, | | | | | | | | |
| | " " plank, | | | | | | | | |
| | " " boards, | | | | | | | | |
| | Hemlock timber, | | | | | | | | |
| | " plank, | | | | | | | | |
| | " boards, | | | | | | | | |
| C. yds. | Field stone, | | | | | | | | |
| " | Quarried stone, | | | | | | | | |

"PROPOSITION for procuring and delivering the following named materials, tools and other implements for the canal, all of which are to be of the quality below stated, and in accordance with the specifications and bills this day exhibited, and to be delivered in good order at the time and place hereinafter mentioned.

| Quantity. | Name of article. | Price. | Amount. | Quality and description. | Time of delivery. | Place of delivery. |
|---|---|---|---|---|---|---|
| | Axes, | | | | | |
| | Augers, | | | | | |
| | Adze, | | | | | |
| | Blocks (teakle), | | | | | |
| | Blasting tools, | | | | | |
| | Brushes (paint), | | | | | |
| | Branding irons, | | | | | |
| | Crowbars, | | | | | |
| | Chains, | | | | | |
| | Chains (draft), | | | | | |
| | Chains (cable), | | | | | |
| | Chisels, | | | | | |
| | Caulking irons, | | | | | |
| | Chests (tool), | | | | | |
| | Drills, | | | | | |
| | Dogs (iron), | | | | | |
| | Files, | | | | | |
| | Frames (paddle), | | | | | |
| | Guages, | | | | | |

| Quantity. | Name of article. | Price. | Amount. | Quality and description. | Time of delivery. | Place of delivery. |
|---|---|---|---|---|---|---|
| | Gimblets, | | | | | |
| | Hoes, | | | | | |
| | Hammers and sledge, | | | | | |
| | Hooks (cant), | | | | | |
| | Hooks (snub), | | | | | |
| | Iron (wrought), | | | | | |
| | Iron (cast), | | | | | |
| | Jugs and cans (oil), | | | | | |
| | Lamps, | | | | | |
| | Lamp fillers, | | | | | |
| | Lanterns, | | | | | |
| | Levels, | | | | | |
| | Levers, | | | | | |
| | Mauls and beetles, | | | | | |
| | Machine (sawing), | | | | | |
| | Nails, | | | | | |
| | Paddle gates, for locks, | | | | | |
| | Padlocks, | | | | | |
| | Picks, | | | | | |
| | Pike poles, | | | | | |
| | Pinch bars, | | | | | |
| | Poles (gin), | | | | | |
| | Ploughs, | | | | | |
| | Pumps, | | | | | |
| | Rakes, | | | | | |
| | Saws, | | | | | |
| | Scythes, | | | | | |
| | Scrapers, | | | | | |
| | Screws, | | | | | |
| | Spike, | | | | | |
| | Shovels, | | | | | |
| | Shaves, | | | | | |
| | Shave horse, | | | | | |
| | Shackle bars, | | | | | |
| | Sledges, | | | | | |
| | Squares, | | | | | |
| | Stones (grind), | | | | | |
| | Stoves, | | | | | |
| | Snaths and irons, | | | | | |
| | Timber hooks, | | | | | |
| | Tongs (blacksmith's), | | | | | |
| | Tow-line, | | | | | |
| | Whiffletrees, | | | | | |
| | Wrenches, | | | | | |
| | OTHER ARTICLES, viz :- | | | | | |

" All blanks are to be filled opposite the articles required to be proposed for.

" PROPOSITION for constructing and delivering the following named boats and other articles, for the canal, all of which are to be of the quality and description below stated, and according to the specifications this day exhibited, and to be delivered in good order, at the place and at the time hereinafter mentioned.

| Number of articles. | Name of article. | Price of each. | Description of article. | Place of delivery. | Time of delivery. |
|---|---|---|---|---|---|
| | Boat, ---------------- | | | | |
| | Ice breaker,----------- | | | | |
| | Under-water excavator,- | | | | |
| | Pile driver, ----------- | | | | |
| | Capstan, ------------- | | | | |
| | Windlass, ------------ | | | | |
| | Ladder,-------------- | | | | |
| | Wheel-barrows, ------- | | | | |
| | Wheels for barrows, --- | | | | |
| | OTHER ARTICLES, viz : | | | | |

" *Form to be attached to and to form part of each of the propositions to be given out.*

" The undersigned hereby propose to the superintendent of repairs of the section of the canal, to procure and deliver in good order, at the several places and on or before the time specified in the above proposition, all of the materials, tools and other implements therein mentioned, which materials, tools and other implements shall be of approved quality and workmanship, and in all respects according to the description of each contained in the above proposition, and in the bill and specifications furnished and this day exhibited by the aforesaid superintendent; and on the acceptance of this proposal, do hereby bind to enter into a written contract with the canal commissioners, at such time as shall be required by them, or either of them, and give the required bond and surety, signed by and at least two other responsible persons, for the delivery of said materials, tools and other implements, as aforesaid, for the consideration and at the prices mentioned in the foregoing proposition.

" Dated at , on the day of , 185 .

" *Guarantee.*

" We, the undersigned, for value received, hereby engage, and by these presents do guarantee to the canal commissioners of the State of New-York, that , who ha made the foregoing propositions for procuring and delivering the materials, tools and other implements therein mentioned, shall, on the acceptance of said proposal, and at such time and place as may be required by said commissioners, enter into written contract with them or their successors in office, and give the bond and surety therein mentioned, for the faithful performance of the terms and conditions of said proposal.

[L. S.]
[L. S.]
[L. S.]

"*The following form is to be used by the superintendent in making the semi-annual estimates.*

"Estimate and statement of materials, tools and all other implements required for the repairs of the section of the canal, extending from to , a distance of miles, during the six months ending on the day of , 185 .

| Quantity. | Kind of material, and for what purpose to be applied. | Estima'd price. | Amount. | Total. |
|---|---|---|---|---|
| | Feet bd. meas. W. oak, for------- | | | |
| | " " " pine, 2d quality, for ----------------------- | | | |
| | Feet bd. meas. hemlock, for ------ | | | |
| | C. yards of , size field stone, for slope wall,-------------- | | | |
| | *Lock No. 1, at* | | | |
| | Ft. bd. meas. W. oak, for-------- | | | |
| | " " " pine, for-------- | | | |
| | " " hemlock, for-------- | | | |
| | Pounds wrought iron, for-------- | | | |
| | " cast " for-------- | | | |
| | C. yards stone, for-------------- | | | |
| | Barrels cement, for ------------ | | | |

"To be continued in like manner until all structures are included that require repairs.

"*Commissioner's certificate of materials required to be obtained by the superintendent before advertising.*

"I certify that I have recently examined into the condition of the , canal, mentioned in the heading of the foregoing estimate of , superintendent of repairs of said , and into the condition of all the mechanical structures thereon, and am of the opinion that the kind and quality of the several materials, tools and other implements, included in said estimate, will be necessary for use in the repairs of said section during the term therein specified.

"Dated at , this day of , 185 .

"*Acting Commissioner on the division of the canals embracing the section above mentioned.*"

### *Annual Report of Property in charge of Superintendents.*

You are required to make an annual report, giving a schedule of all the property belonging to the state on the line of canal under your charge. This will require you to keep a memorandum of every article purchased for the use of the state, and of all tools or implements which are worn out, broken or lost, in order that you may, on the 1st day of January in each year, render a satisfactory account of the property on hand, compared with the previous schedule, and the purchases between the periods of making the two reports.

### *Old Materials—how disposed of and accounted for.*

Whenever aqueducts or other structures are repaired, the utmost caution and strictness should be observed in relation to the old materials. These materials, of every description, if not necessary to be preserved for the use of the state, should be sold to the highest bidder, after giving reasonable public notice of the sale. The proceeds of such sale should be reported and accounted for at the close of the sixty days in which the sale is made. And you should, in thus reporting it, specify the time and place when such sale was made and the notice that was given thereof. The superintendent should not himself be interested in any purchases of public property sold on the line of the canal.

Whenever paddle-gates, or any of the iron work connected with the locks, are replaced, the lock-tender should be held responsible for the safe keeping of the old article, which, if it cannot be repaired and used, should be disposed of by the superintendent for the benefit of the state, and accounted for by him.

### *Suits for Penalties, &c.*

The superintendents, in a great variety of cases, are authorized to sue in the name of the people for penalties for violations of the canal law and the regulations of the canal board. Where the superintendent is sued or commences a suit before a justice, if the suit is to be carried to a higher court by either party, a full statement of the case should be made and sent to the auditor, in order that the advice of the attorney-general may be obtained before a heavy bill of costs has been made for the state to pay. Claims for costs, unless a sum sufficient for the purpose is recovered, cannot be paid until they are examined and allowed by the commissioners of the canal fund, as required by law.

### *Breaches.*

Whenever there is a breach in the canal, you should immediately give notice of it to the auditor as well as the commissioner. If money will be required to enable you to pay off the hands employed on the breach, you should state the facts in your notice to the auditor. As soon as the breach is repaired, the auditor should be informed of it, and of the expense incurred. This is desirable, as well on account of having authentic information in relation to the condition of the navigation, as on account of the expenditure for the repair.

Timely examinations of the structures connected with the public works, and unremitting vigilance on the part of the superintendent and those employed under him, may, in almost every case, prevent breaches. Where they take place, and a heavy expense is incurred by the state, and the trade of the canals is interrupted, it is important that the superintendent and those under him should be enabled to show that the occurrence is not attributable to any neglect on their part.

Last season was one peculiarly unfortunate in regard to breaches, and it is believed that the most part, if not all of them, could have been avoided by proper care and attention on the part of the superintendents and their subordinates. With proper watching and regulation of the levels, breaches in the canals seldom, if ever, need occur; and you will be expected to use every means within your power to protect against them. The canal board, believing that they are generally more the result of negligence than unavoidable accident, have directed me to notify you that they will hold each superintendent to a rigid accountability for any breaches that may occur upon his section, and will act upon the principle that a superintendent who cannot, except under very extraordinary circumstances, protect the canal from breaches, is *incompetent* for the charge.

### *Publication of Monthly Abstract.*

The law passed in March, 1853, being chapter 52 of the Laws of that year, which requires you to publish monthly abstracts of your disbursements, provides that "the expense of such publication shall not exceed the sum of fifteen dollars, to be regulated and fixed by the auditor of the canal department." Taking the experience of the publications for six months, in twenty-five different newspapers, and after making diligent inquiry of various papers, city and country, I have concluded to fix the rate of compensation, applicable to all papers, at seventy-five cents *for each sixteen lines of an ordinary newspaper column*, which, for the Evening Journal, Argus and Atlas, of this city, is called a square. Experience thus far shows that at that rate of compensation the expense of three-fourths of the publications would not average more than about $9 per month, while the average of the largest would scarcely exceed the $15 per month.

It must, of course, be understood that you cannot pay more than $15 for a single month. If, at the rate fixed, it would amount to more than $15, and no paper will publish it, then you are to file it as directed by the law.

Almost all the papers follow the form prescribed, and confine the publication to the width of a column. A few occupy the width of two columns. In such cases, the pay will be for only one-half the space occupied and at the rate mentioned.

As the publications at some of the offices will, during some of the months, exceed the $15, and other months probably fall short, and it appearing more desirable that the abstracts during the expensive months should be published than the others, I conclude that the true construction of the law will authorize you to contract with any paper for the publication of your monthly abstract, for the year, at the rate of compensation by the square above specified, but such compensation not to exceed in the aggregate, for the twelve monthly insertions, $180 ; and your accounts for printing will be audited upon such basis, in case you forward to this department a written agreement on the part of the proprietor of the paper to publish on such terms for the year.

### *In Relation to Money.*

You are prohibited, by a resolution of the canal board, from being the agent of any bank, either for the exchange and circulation of its money, or for any other purpose whatever. You have no right to make exchanges of the money belonging to the state for personal gain or for the accommodation of any bank. The state will furnish you with current money, and the money received by you should be paid to those who render service to the state.

You should not retain in your hands the money belonging to the workmen, or any of them, although they may request you to do it for their use and benefit. If any of them desire to deposit their money with you for safe keeping, you should decline receiving it; being the agent of the state, you cannot accept these trusts from those who work for the state without creating in their minds the belief that in this transaction, also, you are in some degree acting in your official capacity, and that the state ought to be responsible for your acts.

You have a high responsibility cast upon you; and the interests of the state, as well as the interests of those who navigate the canals, are to be affected favorably or unfavorably by the manner in which you discharge your duties. You cannot do justice to the public or to your own character without being constantly on the line of the canal, and devoting your whole energies to the public service.

Money is placed in your hands, to an immense amount, with the confident reliance that you will faithfully expend it in paying those who have furnished materials for the canal or rendered service to the state. Beyond the amount of your own salary, which you are allowed to receive every two months, you should not permit yourself to use a dollar of the public money for private purposes, under any pretence whatever.

### *Clerks, &c.*

Such superintendents as are allowed clerks will appoint such clerks subject to removal by the canal commissioner, who will also determine the amount to be paid them for their services.

You will receive from your predecessor, the late superintendent of repairs, all books, blanks, papers and other property belonging to the state, which he may have in possession, rendering a receipt therefor, and send a copy of such receipt to this office.

You will carefully preserve all circulars, pamphlets and printed directions which you may from time to time receive from this office, and carefully place the same on file.

Yours. respectfully,

M. SCHOONMAKER, *Auditor.*

[Vouchers and Check Rolls should be entered invariably in the order of their dates. Both sides of the sheet are to be written upon. No. 7 is to be equal to the footings of all the columns, from 2 to 6 inclusive.]

## ( FORM. )

AN ABSTRACT OF EXPENDITURES *by A. B., Superintendent of Repairs upon the Canal, and having charge of miles of said canal, extending from*

*for the sixty days, commencing on the 1st of February, and ending on the 31st March,* 1854.

| No. of Voucher. | Date money was paid. | To whom paid. | For what Expenditure | 1. Monthly entry of Lock-tending and Check Rolls. | 2. Lock tending. | 3. Labor. | 4. Materials. | 5. Merchants' and Mechanics' bills. | 6. Miscellaneous. | 7. Total. |
|---|---|---|---|---|---|---|---|---|---|---|
| | 1854. | | | | | | | | | |
| 1 | Feb'y 10, | C. D. | Timber, | | | | $8 44 | | | $8 44 |
| 2 | " 11, | E. F. | Blacksmithing, | | | | | $4 37 | | 4 37 |
| 3 | " 15, | G. H. | Stone, | | | | 200 00 | | | 200 00 |
| 4 | " 18, | I. J. | Tools, | | | | | 80 00 | | 80 00 |
| 5 | March 1, | K. L. | Tending Lock No. 1, April, | 30 00 | | | | | | |
| 6 | " 1, | M. N. | " " " 2, " | 30 00 | | | | | | |
| 7 | " 1, | O. P. | " " " 3, " | 30 00 | | | | | | |
| 8 | " 1, | Q. R. | " " " 4 & 5, April, | 60 00 | | | | | | |
| | | | | | $150 00 | | | | | 150 00 |
| 9 | " 1, | S. T. | Check Roll, April, | 127 62 | | | | | | |
| 10 | " 1, | U. V. | " " | 200 50 | | | | | | |
| 11 | " 1, | D. C. | " " | 247 00 | | | | | | |
| | | | | | | $575 12 | | | | 575 12 |
| 12 | April 1, | F. C. | Timber, | | | | 57 00 | | | 57 00 |
| 13 | " 1, | H. G. | Gravel, | | | | 20 00 | | | 20 00 |
| 14 | " 1, | J. I. | Merchant's Bill, | | | | | 90 00 | | 90 00 |
| 15 | " 1, | L. K. | Damage to land, | | | | | | $5 00 | 5 00 |
| 16 | " 1, | K. L. | Tending Lock No. 1, May, | 30 00 | | | | | | |
| 17 | " 1, | M. N. | " " " 2, " | 30 00 | | | | | | |
| 18 | " 1, | O. P. | " " " 3, " | 30 00 | | | | | | |
| 19 | " 1, | Q. R. | " " " 4 & 5, May, | 60 00 | | | | | | |
| | | | | | 150 00 | | | | | 150 00 |
| 20 | " 1, | S. T. | Check Roll, May, | 350 00 | | | | | | |
| 21 | " 1, | U. V. | " " | 520 00 | | | | | | |
| 22 | " 1, | D. E. | " " | 230 00 | | | | | | |
| | | | | | | 1,100 00 | | | | 1,100 00 |
| | | | | | $300 00 | $1,675 12 | $285 44 | $174 37 | $5 00 | $2,489 93 |
| 23 | " 1, | A. B. | Superintendent, 2 months' pay, April and May, | | | | | | | 125 00 |
| 24 | " 2, | R. S. | Clerk, " " " | | | | | | | 60 00 |
| | | | | | | | | | | $2.624 93 |

| | | |
|---|---|---|
| Balance from last abstract due the state (or due me, as the case may be), | | $40 00 |
| Deposited since that abstract, my drafts on the auditor of the canal department, to my credit in the Bank, | | 2,920 00 |
| | | $2,960 00 |
| Expended as per present abstract, | | 2,624 93 |
| Balance, | | $335 07 |
| Of this balance there is in bank, | $300 00 | |
| " " " hand, | 35 07 | |
| Total in "bank" and in "hand," equal to "balance" above, | | $335 07 |

C. D., *Superintendent of Canal Repairs.*

Dated this 2d day of April, 1854.

STATE OF NEW-YORK, } *ss.*
*County of* }

, superintendent of canal repairs, having charge of the line of canal specified in the above abstract, doth solemnly swear that the foregoing is a true abstract of all the vouchers, taken by him as such superintendent, for the days ending on the day of , 185 ; and doth further swear that the money specified in the several receipts, of which the above is an abstract (except those marked "A" on the back as having been paid by agents), has been actually paid as specified in said receipts, in cash or by check on the Bank; and further, that all the receipts, not specially excepted, were each and every of them filled up as they now appear, before they were signed; and he doth further swear that, according to the best of his knowledge and belief, all the labor has been performed, services rendered and materials furnished for the benefit of the state, and the state alone, and at as fair and reasonable prices as the same could be procured; and further swears that all fines, penalties and forfeitures collected, and the sales of public property made during the period aforesaid, on the line of canal under his charge, are, according to the best of his knowledge and belief, correctly entered on the said abstract.

C. D., *Superintendent.*

Subscribed and sworn to before me, this }
day of , 185 . }

A. B., *Canal Commissioner.*

[In the absence of the canal commissioner, the oath may be taken before any judge or commissioner ]

I certify that I have examined the preceding abstract, and the vouchers of which it is an abstract, amounting to dollars cents; that the several disbursements specified therein were made under my direction on the canal or for repairs necessary to be made thereon, and that I believe such disbursements were proper and reasonable, and have been made as charged in the said abstract and vouchers.

(Signed) A. B., *Canal Commissioner upon that part of the canal described in the heading of the above abstract.*

Dated 6th day of April, 1854.

NOTES.—Should a voucher contain articles or matter that would come under two or more of the above heads, put the true amount under each head, and the total in the total column.

The column before the one headed "lock-tending," is intended for the entry of lock-tending and check rolls for a month, to get at the footing of each for that period, to be carried under the appropriate heads.

The above "form" is intended to show the superintendents how they are to fill up their abstracts to be sent to the canal department. It is expected that this "*form*" will be always used by every superintendent as a guide in making up their abstracts.

www.ingramcontent.com/pod-product-compliance
Lightning Source LLC
LaVergne TN
LVHW011143110826
845150LV00008B/2490

* 9 7 8 1 4 1 8 1 9 2 9 1 4 *